W9-ANF-165

U.S. PRESIDENTIAL ELECTIONS: HOW THEY WORK

PRESIDENTIAL PRIMARIES AND CAUCUSES

DANIELLE HAYNES

PowerKiDS
press

New York

Published in 2020 by The Rosen Publishing Group, Inc.
29 East 21st Street, New York, NY 10010

First Edition

Editor: Rachel Gintner
Book Design: Tanya Dellaccio

Photo Credits: Cover Hero Images/Getty Images; p. 4 YURI GRIPAS/AFP/Getty Images; p. 5 Bloomberg/ Getty Images; p. 7 (top) Darren McCollester/Getty Images News/Getty Images; p. 7 (bottom) Smith Collection/Gado/Archive Photos/Getty Images; p. 9 (top) Joe Sohm/Visions of America/Universal Images Group/Getty Images; pp. 9 (bottom), 15 (top), 22 ROBYN BECK/AFP/Getty Images; p. 11 BestStockFoto/Shutterstock.com; p. 12 https://commons.wikimedia.org/wiki/File:James_ Madison(cropped)(c).jpg; p. 13 (top) Brendan Hoffman/Getty Images News/Getty Images; p. 13 (bottom) Joshua Lott/Getty Images News/Getty Images; p. 15 (bottom) Eric Thayer/Getty Images News/Getty Images; p. 16 Craig F. Walker/Denver Post/Getty Images; pp. 17, 21 Scott Olson/Getty Images News/ Getty Images; p. 19 (top) MCT/Tribune News Service/Getty Images; p. 19 (bottom) Charles Ommanney/ Getty Images News/Getty Images; p. 23 John Sommers II/Getty Images News/Getty Images; p. 25 Justin Sullivan/Getty Images News/Getty Images; p. 27 (top) Pool/Getty Images News/Getty Images; p. 27 (bottom) Mark Reinstein/Corbis Historical/Getty Images; p. 29 MediaNews Group/Orange County Register/Getty Images.

Library of Congress Cataloging-in-Publication Data

Names: Haynes, Danielle.
Title: Presidential primaries and caucuses / Danielle Haynes.
Description: New York : PowerKids Press, 2020. | Series: U.S. presidential elections: how they work | Includes glossary and index.
Identifiers: ISBN 9781725310988 (pbk.) | ISBN 9781725311008 (library bound) | ISBN 9781725310995 (6 pack)
Subjects: LCSH: Presidents–United States–Election–Juvenile literature. | Presidents–United States–Nomina-tion–Juvenile literature. | Primaries–United States–Juvenile literature.
Classification: LCC JK524.H374 2020 | DDC 324.60973 –dc23

Manufactured in the United States of America

CPSIA Compliance Information: Batch # CWPK20. For Further Information contact Rosen Publishing, New York, New York at 1-800-237-9932.

CONTENTS

PRIMARY SEASON

Though Americans go to the polls one day every four years to vote for a new president, elections are actually a yearlong process that involves multiple rounds of voting. The election of a new U.S. president includes two separate parts—primary season during the spring, followed by the general election in November. For Americans in most states, this means you likely head to the polls twice during the election year.

Voters may go to the polls two times to vote in an election year— once during their state's primary and a second time on Election Day.

During primary season, which runs from February to June, each state holds either primary elections or caucuses. These events are the way major political parties decide who they'll nominate to run for president on Election Day. Without nominations, dozens of candidates could be on the final **ballot** in November.

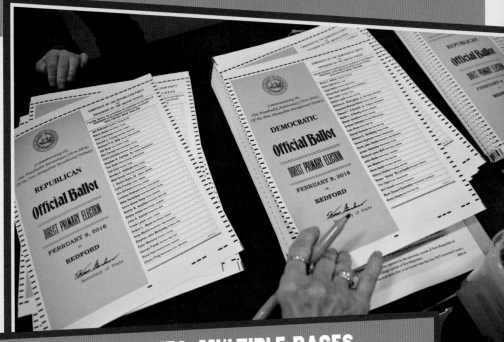

MULTIPLE PARTIES, MULTIPLE RACES

THE MAJOR PARTIES HOLD THEIR OWN SEPARATE PRIMARIES OR CAUCUSES IN EACH STATE, SO CANDIDATES INITIALLY ONLY RUN AGAINST MEMBERS OF THEIR OWN PARTY. THIS IS BECAUSE PRIMARY SEASON IS A CONTEST TO FIND THE BEST CANDIDATE WITHIN EACH PARTY. LATER, THAT CANDIDATE WILL RUN AGAINST CANDIDATES FROM OTHER PARTIES IN THE GENERAL ELECTION. THE TWO MAJOR PARTIES—DEMOCRATIC AND REPUBLICAN—DOMINATE U.S. POLITICS. HOWEVER, SMALLER PARTIES ALSO HOLD PRIMARIES TO NOMINATE CANDIDATES, INCLUDING THE GREEN PARTY AND LIBERTARIAN PARTY.

WHY WE NEED PRIMARIES AND CAUCUSES

If political parties didn't use primaries and caucuses to pick which candidate to nominate, there could be dozens of people on the ballot running for president. For example, by spring 2019, more than 20 Democrats announced they planned to run for president in 2020! With so many candidates, it might be hard for voters to decide who to support.

It also increases the chances that no one candidate wins a majority of the support on Election Day because too many candidates would split votes. If that happens, the House of Representatives, one of two bodies in Congress, elects the president.

So, primaries and caucuses—which are used to narrow the number of candidates—are a key way for Americans to make sure their voices are heard throughout the election process.

In 2008, many Democrats ran for president, but after several months of campaigning and debate, all but one lost the nomination. Barack Obama won that nomination, and later, the presidency.

THE STRANGE CASE OF THE 1824 ELECTION

THE OUTCOME OF THE 1824 ELECTION RESULTED IN THE CREATION OF PRIMARIES AND CAUCUSES TO NOMINATE A PRESIDENT. THAT YEAR, FOUR CANDIDATES RAN FOR PRESIDENT AND NO ONE WON A MAJORITY OF VOTES, WHICH WAS REQUIRED TO WIN. IF NO ONE WINS A MAJORITY ON ELECTION DAY, U.S. LAW SAYS THE HOUSE OF REPRESENTATIVES MUST SELECT THE PRESIDENT. THEY PICKED JOHN QUINCY ADAMS TO BE PRESIDENT EVEN THOUGH HE HAD FEWER VOTES THAN ANDREW JACKSON.

TALLY OF 1824 ELECTORAL COLLEGE VOTE

WHAT'S A PRIMARY?

In some states, political parties hold primary elections to pick who they'll nominate to be president. Primaries are similar to Election Day in November. Voters go to the polls to vote for their favorite candidate. The polls are open for several hours on primary election day, allowing most voters to participate at a time that's convenient for them.

Primaries are different from Election Day in that each political party holds its own contest in each state, and voters must pick which party's primary they want to vote in. Some states hold closed primaries, meaning only voters who are registered with a particular party can vote in that party's primary. Other states allow open primaries—anyone can vote in either the Democratic or Republican contest, but not both.

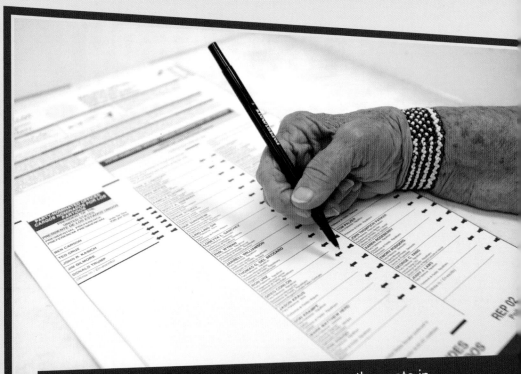

People vote in primary elections the same way they vote in the general election, by selecting candidates on a ballot.

WHAT ABOUT CAUCUSES?

Caucuses are more **complicated** than primaries. In this process, party members meet at a specific time to talk about candidates and pick the nominee. Any party member can participate, but not as many do because fewer caucus meetings are held and the meetings take much longer than primaries.

Instead of using ballots, caucus-goers either raise their hands or group together to vote. Undecided participants form their own group.

The caucus-goers then debate and try to persuade undecided voters to support their candidate. Participants can even switch sides!

Republican Party caucuses are winner-take-all contests, meaning the candidate who receives the most votes wins all votes. Democratic Party caucuses are **proportional**, so a candidate who gets 60 percent of the vote during the caucuses will end up with that same percent of votes.

In some cases, caucus-goers move to one side of a room to show their vote.

11

BEFORE THERE WERE PRIMARIES

In the country's early days, Congress nominated candidates for president instead of holding modern primaries or caucuses. Some people disagreed with this because the Constitution says Congress and the president must operate as separate branches of the government—one cannot be **beholden** to the other. This problem was illustrated in 1812, when lawmakers said President James Madison must declare war on Britain if he wanted to be nominated for a second term.

PATH TO THE PRESIDENCY

PRESIDENT JAMES MADISON CAME CLOSE TO LOSING THE NOMINATION FOR HIS SECOND TERM IN OFFICE TO NEW YORK CITY MAYOR DEWITT CLINTON.

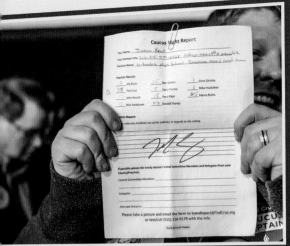

Many presidential candidates, such as Bernie Sanders, hold caucus nights to continue advocating for the separation of government branches and oversight.

In the mid-19th century, parties began holding caucuses to select candidates without Congress's involvement, but only party insiders participated. States began to switch from caucuses to primaries to encourage more voters to participate. Primaries are now more popular than caucuses—12 states held caucuses in 2016, and that number is expected to decline in 2020.

THE ROLE OF DELEGATES

Primaries and caucuses don't use a popular vote to determine nominees. In a popular vote, a person is elected or nominated based on who won the majority of all votes; one person equals one vote.

Instead, primary season uses delegates, who represent the whole population of the state. For instance, in 2016, more than 5 million people voted in the California Democratic primaries, but the state awarded 551 delegates to the top 2 winners. Each state has a certain number of delegates. States with higher populations tend to have more.

The results of the primaries and caucuses determine who the delegates vote for in each party's **convention** at the end of primary season. The candidate with the most delegates from all states wins the nomination.

National conventions are often festive events and some delegates wear patriotic clothing, hats, and pins. ▶

WHO ARE THE DELEGATES?

DELEGATES AREN'T JUST VOTES, THEY'RE ACTUAL PEOPLE. THESE PEOPLE ATTEND THEIR PARTY'S NATIONAL CONVENTION IN THE SUMMER AND CAST THEIR VOTE FOR A CANDIDATE BASED ON THE RESULTS OF PRIMARIES AND CAUCUSES. THESE PEOPLE ARE USUALLY STRONGLY INVOLVED IN PARTY ACTIVITIES AND ARE LOCAL LEADERS OR CAMPAIGN WORKERS FOR A PARTICULAR CANDIDATE. EACH STATE HAS ITS OWN PROCESS TO SELECT WHO GETS TO BE A DELEGATE.

SUPERDELEGATES

The Democratic Party also has people called superdelegates. These are high-ranking party members, including congressional representatives, governors, former presidents, and former vice presidents.

Superdelegates, similarly to delegates, cast votes for candidates at the nominating conventions. Unlike delegates, they can vote for whichever candidate they want. They are not pledged to vote for the winner of their state's primaries or caucuses.

SUPERDELEGATE:
2008

Critics say the use of superdelegates gives high-ranking Democrats too much power. The party changed its rules in 2018, only allowing superdelegates to vote if a majority can't be reached with regular delegates first.

In 2016, more than 700 of the Democratic Party's 4,763 delegates were superdelegates, giving high-ranking party insiders great influence over who became the nominee. To limit that power, starting in 2020, superdelegates can only vote at the Democratic National Convention if no candidate receives a majority of regular delegates.

Republicans also have superdelegates, but there aren't as many, and they're required to vote for the candidate who won their state's primary or caucus.

CAMPAIGNING

The biggest goal for candidates during primary season is to win as many delegates as possible. In 2016, Democrats needed 2,382 delegates and superdelegates out of a total 4,763 possible to win the nomination. Republicans needed 1,237 delegates out of a possible 2,472 to win.

To win those delegates, candidates campaign across the country, paying special attention to states right before their primaries and caucuses are held. The candidates travel to dozens of cities and towns to give speeches and explain their views on political issues. They meet with voters and leaders, whom they try to persuade to vote for them.

Candidates also take part in televised debates with fellow party members to answer questions and tell voters how they'll make a better president than their competitors.

PATH TO THE PRESIDENCY

EVEN THOUGH PRIMARY SEASON BEGINS IN FEBRUARY, SOME CANDIDATES HAVE ALREADY BEEN CAMPAIGNING FOR MORE THAN A YEAR. MANY PRESIDENTIAL CANDIDATES ANNOUNCE THEIR PLANS TO RUN TWO SPRINGS BEFORE ELECTION DAY.

Presidential candidates travel around the country giving speeches and shaking hands with potential supporters.

WHY ARE IOWA AND NEW HAMPSHIRE SO IMPORTANT?

Among the most important days on the primary season calendar are the Iowa caucuses and the New Hampshire primaries. A win in either state can help boost a candidate's profile and **media coverage** because they're scheduled earlier than other states', so candidates spend a lot of time campaigning there. In return for support, residents sometimes expect candidates to back their **special interests**.

When the two states realized how much influence they could **wield** over candidates, each passed laws saying they would hold the first contests each presidential election year.

Some critics say this gives the small states too much power even though they represent a small number of Americans. Iowa had 30 Republican and 51 Democratic delegates in 2016. New Hampshire had 23 Republican and 32 Democratic delegates.

STATES HOLD PRIMARIES ON TUESDAYS AND SATURDAYS THROUGHOUT THE FIRST SIX MONTHS OF THE YEAR. SOME STATES, SUCH AS NEVADA AND SOUTH CAROLINA, HOLD THEIR REPUBLICAN CONTEST ON A DIFFERENT DAY FROM THEIR DEMOCRATIC CONTEST, BUT MOST HOLD BOTH ON THE SAME DAY.

Even though Donald Trump didn't win the most delegates in the Iowa caucuses in 2016, he still won the Republican nomination and then the presidency.

SUPER TUESDAY

Another big day on the calendar is Super Tuesday. While the Iowa caucuses and New Hampshire primaries award relatively few delegates, Super Tuesday is the first day of primary season when candidates can expect to grab hundreds of delegates. This day can make or break campaigns.

Super Tuesday is usually in February or early March. In 2016, it involved 13 states and territories, with 661 Republican and 865 Democratic delegates up for grabs. The 2020 primary season will place even more importance on the day because California, which has the most delegates of all states, will hold its primaries on Super Tuesday.

Media organizations have used the term "Super Tuesday II" or "Super Saturday" to describe other days when there are multiple primaries and caucuses held at the same time.

Super Tuesday is a busy day in the United States, when more than a dozen states hold primaries and caucuses.

2016 KENTUCKY
PRESIDENTIAL CAUCUS BALLOT
CHOOSE ONE CANDIDATE BY FILLING IN THE CIRCLE.

○ TED CRUZ

○ MARCO RUBIO

○ JOHN R. KASICH

○ DONALD J. TRUMP

○ RAND PAUL

○ JEB BUSH

○ DR. BEN CARSON

○ MIKE HUCKABEE

○ CARLY FIORINA

○ RICK SANTORUM

○ CHRIS CHRISTIE

○ UNCOMMITTED

NARROWING THE FIELD

As primary season progresses, presidential candidates gradually **accumulate** delegates who are pledged to vote for them at the national conventions held in the summer. When there are several candidates in a given political party, some will start to drop out of the race when they realize there's little chance for them to earn enough delegates to win the nomination.

When a candidate drops out, they can choose to **endorse** a former rival in the race. If they do this, the delegates who were committed to the departing candidate, can then pledge to vote for the candidate they endorsed.

By the time the national conventions are held, it's usually obvious who has the delegates needed to win the nominations, and all but one or two candidates have dropped out.

Though several candidates ran during the Republican primary in 2016, by the time the Republican National Convention took place in July, only one remained—Donald Trump.

THE CONVENTIONS

Primary season ends with the national conventions, when the parties formally nominate a presidential candidate. Each major party holds its own convention, and even some minor ones, such as the Green and Libertarian parties, gather to make nominations. The events last a few days.

Delegates attend the conventions—which are held in different cities every four years—and cast their votes based on the results of their state's primary or caucus. The candidate who receives the majority of delegate votes wins their party's nomination.

If no candidate receives a majority of delegates, the party holds another round of voting, and pledged delegates may be released to vote for a different candidate. This is when Democratic superdelegates are allowed to vote.

Thousands of people—in addition to the delegates—attend the national conventions to hear speeches about the party's **platform**.

FRONT-LOADING

Not everyone agrees that the United States' system of primaries and caucuses is the best way to nominate presidential candidates. Officials in some states, unhappy that Iowa and New Hampshire have so much influence over candidates, have tried to hold their contests earlier in the year. This is called front-loading. Super Tuesday came about as a result of front-loading.

To discourage this practice—and to protect Iowa and New Hampshire's first-in-the-nation statuses—the major parties have threatened to strip states of their delegates if they hold contests too early in the year. In 2008, Florida and Michigan lost some of their Republican and all of their Democratic delegates for holding their primaries in January. Front-loading shortens the primary season and makes it difficult for lesser-known candidates to build support.

For the 2020 election, California moved its election forward, so it falls on Super Tuesday.

NOW VOTE!

Like many countries today, the United States once allowed party leaders to select presidential candidates. But a growing interest in making it a more **democratic** process led to the creation of a system that gave the American people more of a voice in selecting their leadership.

Voter turnout during primary season is relatively low. In 2016, 57.6 million people voted in primaries and caucuses, less than half the number who voted on Election Day. The major parties continue to reform the process to encourage more voters to participate. The Democrats, for example, are pushing more states to hold primaries instead of caucuses.

Voting for a president doesn't just start and end on Election Day in November. When you become old enough, remember that primary day is just as important!

GLOSSARY

accumulate: To gather or increase in amount.

ballot: A sheet of paper or digital screen voters use to
    pick candidates.

beholden: Being required to do something.

complicated: Difficult.

convention: A large meeting of people at a central location.

democratic: Separate from the political party, a government
    by the pople.

endorse: To give your approval to a candidate.

media coverage: The attention news organizations give
    to something.

platform: The policies a person or group of people
    believe in.

proportional: Corresponding in size.

special interests: A group seeking to influence a politician
    or group of politicians on a specific topic.

wield: To have command over something.

INDEX

WEBSITES

Due to the changing nature of Internet links, PowerKids Press has developed an online list of websites related to the subject of this book. This site is updated regularly. Please use this link to access the list: www.powerkidslinks.com/uspe/primaries